D1533739

CELL BIOLOGY

AUBREY STIMOLA

rosen publishing's
rosen
central®

New York

For my sister, Adriana. Boy, did I luck out.

Published in 2011 by The Rosen Publishing Group, Inc.
29 East 21st Street, New York, NY 10010

Library of Congress Cataloging-in-Publication Data

Stimola, Aubrey.
Cell biology / Aubrey Stimola. — 1st ed.
    p. cm. — (Science made simple)
Includes bibliographical references and index.
ISBN 978-1-4488-1234-9 (library binding)
ISBN 978-1-4488-2241-6 (pbk.)
ISBN 978-1-4488-2244-7 (6-pack)
1. Cytology—Juvenile literature. I. Title.
QH582.5.S755 2011
571.6—dc22

                                                                    2010021319

Manufactured in Malaysia

CPSIA Compliance Information: Batch #W11YA: For further information, contact Rosen Publishing, New York, New York, at 1-800-237-9932.

On the cover: The top and bottom images illustrate color-enhanced graphics of human cells.

CONTENTS

INTRODUCTION

There are many kinds of human cells, each of which performs a specific task. In other words, cells can be specialized. Some cells work alone, and some work as a unit with other cells by coming together to form tissues and organs. Some cells in the body are responsible for making bone, the substance from which the skeleton is made. Other cells work together to make muscle tissue, allowing the skeleton to move and the heart to pump blood. Blood, too, is made of specialized cells that can carry oxygen from the lungs to all the organs of the body. Even the skin that covers and protects the body is made of cells.

Cells have a number of different functions in the body, including converting the food we eat into usable energy. This energy is used to make more cells, repair damaged organs and tissues, move muscles, and make proteins. Protein is a substance that the body uses to make some of its components, including hair, bone, skin, and other cells.

In the striated pattern of skeletal muscle, each tiny rectangular area is called a sarcomere. Each sarcomere contains special proteins that work together to help the muscle contract.

Human cells come together to make four primary types of tissue, each with special jobs. Bone, cartilage, tendons, ligaments, fat, and blood are all types of connective tissue. These cells contain strong substances called collagens.

The cells that make up muscle tissue contain special filaments called actin and myosin that allow muscles to contract. Some muscles, like the ones you use to walk and talk, are voluntary—you can move them at your command. Others, like heart muscle, are involuntary. They contract without you thinking about them.

Nerve tissue can create and deliver electrical messages to all parts of the body. Some messages start in the nerve cells of the brain and are sent down the spinal cord and out to the other organs and tissues. Other signals start in the tissues and organs and are carried back to the brain. In this way, the different parts of the body can communicate. Nerve cells have two important parts: the axon and the dendrite. Like an electric cable, the axon sends information away from the cell to other cells and tissues. Like a radio antenna, the dendrite receives information sent from other cells and tissues.

The skin surrounding the body and the membranes around the organs are made up of epithelial tissue. These cells are packed very closely together to form protective barriers.

Humans and other animals aren't the only organisms that have cells. Plants have cells, too. So do fungi, including mold and yeast. Some organisms, including plants and animals, are multicellular—they are made up of many cells. Others are unicellular, meaning that they are made up of only one individual cell. Unicellular organisms, while considered to be less evolved than multicellular organisms, have important roles to play in our lives, both good and bad. These include the bacteria that can sometimes make us ill but that also play a vital role in the production of food, medications, and vaccines, and in the breakdown and recycling of substances into usable nutrients. Our bodies actually serve as a home to several species of bacteria without which we could not survive. For example, bacterial cells that live in our intestines produce vitamin K2, which is important in blood clotting so that when you cut yourself, you stop bleeding.

Cell biology is the field of science that studies the properties of cells, how cells work, what they do, and how they interact with their environment. Understanding how different types of cells function helps us gain insight to other important fields of biology and medicine, including genetics, immunology, cancer research, the aging process, and how we develop from the meeting of sperm and egg into walking, talking, and thinking individuals. Knowledge in these areas can help us prolong our lives by keeping us healthy and preventing or curing illnesses. It can also help us understand how we evolved and might continue to evolve.

1

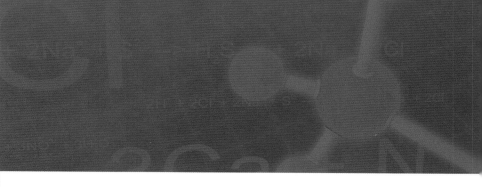

INSIDE A CELL

Human cells are protected and separated from other cells by the cell membrane, a flexible barrier that is semipermeable (allowing for the passage of some particles but not others). The cell membrane surrounds the entire cell and is made of phospholipids. These special molecules each have a spherical head and a long tail. The heads are hydrophilic, or attracted to water, while the tails are hydrophobic, or repelled by water. When placed in water, these molecules arrange themselves so that their heads are immersed in water and their tails are protected from it. Because the environment outside and inside a cell is made mostly of water, this natural tendency results in the formation of a double layer of molecules surrounding and protecting the inside of the cell, keeping its contents together and separate from the environment, much as a fence keeps a flock of sheep in and the wolves out.

The cell membrane also contains several molecules that help control what gets into and out of the cell. We will take a closer look at this later. These proteins often float freely within the membrane, rather than having a fixed position. For this reason, the structure of the cell membrane is often described as a fluid mosaic.

Human cells are filled with cytosol, a gelatinous and nutrient-filled fluid made of 80 percent water. This is where important cellular processes take place. Floating in the cytosol are all the other components of the cell, known as organelles. The collective term for the cytosol, plus all the organelles that are suspended within it, is the cytoplasm. The organelles each have special jobs inside the cell.

THE NUCLEUS

The nucleus is the cellular command center; it dictates all of the cell's activities. All human cells contain a nucleus with the exception of red blood cells, which lose theirs as they mature. The nucleus, too, is surrounded by a protective double membrane that has pores, or openings, through which only certain substances can pass. The nucleus contains more than 6 feet (1.8 meters) of deoxyribonucleic acid, or DNA. DNA, like an enormous cookbook, contains millions of recipes in the form of genes. Just as a chef can create dishes from recipes, the genes in DNA can be translated into instructions that tell

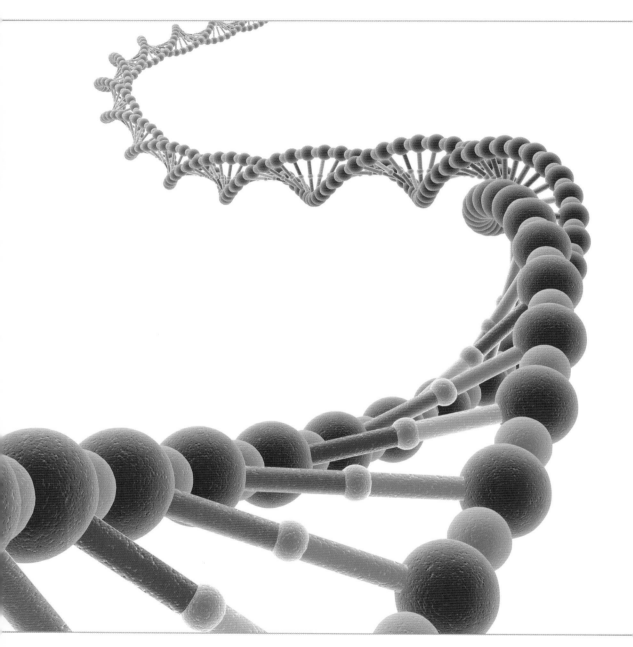

The DNA double helix is made of two interlocking strands of four bases, phosphate groups, and sugars that wind together like a spiral staircase.

the cell what kinds of proteins to make and what to do with them. How does all that DNA fit in your cells? This massive amount of information is first coiled into threadlike chromatin and then into forty-six highly organized chromosomes.

All the cells in your body contain the exact same DNA and genes. Depending on the cell type, however, only certain recipes, or genes, are available for translation. The unused genes are tightly packed in coils. For example, liver cells have to make certain proteins and perform certain functions that skin cells do not. Both cell types contain the same genes, but the liver cells have easy access to certain recipes that skin cells will never have reason to make.

One way to understand this is to imagine an enormous book containing all the information in the universe. If you were a doctor, it would make sense for you to bookmark only the sections of that book important to your job. However, if you were an auto mechanic, that same information would be a waste of your time and energy. For that reason, you would bookmark different sections of the book to easily access the information that you need.

PROKARYOTES, EUKARYOTES, AND THE ENDOSYMBIOTIC THEORY

The cells of all animals, plants, fungi, and algae have a nucleus to house and protect their DNA. Bacterial cells, however, have no nucleus. Their DNA exists in one long strand condensed into a nucleoid with no protective membrane. Bacterial DNA, therefore, is much more vulnerable to damage.

Organisms whose cells have a nucleus and other membrane-bound organelles are called eukaryotes. With a few exceptions, organisms whose cells do not have a nucleus or membrane-bound organelles are called prokaryotes.

Members of the kingdom Monera, which includes all bacteria, are the only prokaryotic organisms. Which came first—eukaryotes or prokaryotes? One theory is that long ago, a prokaryotic cell ingested another smaller prokaryotic cell. Instead of killing it, the cell benefited from the presence of the smaller cell. As it continued to function inside the larger cell, it served a role for it. Over time, the two merged cells became dependent on each other, developing a symbiotic relationship—one needed the other to survive. It is thought that these ingested cells later became the organelles, including the mitochondria and chloroplasts.

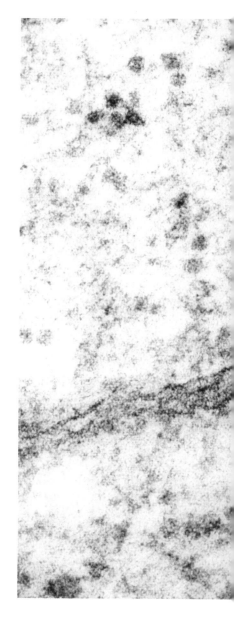

The thin brown lines shown here represent the double membrane surrounding the nucleus. The small purple circles outside the nucleus are ribosomes, the organelles that translate messenger RNA into proteins.

Ribosomes

When a cell needs to make a certain protein to perform a certain activity, the information on the gene that codes for that

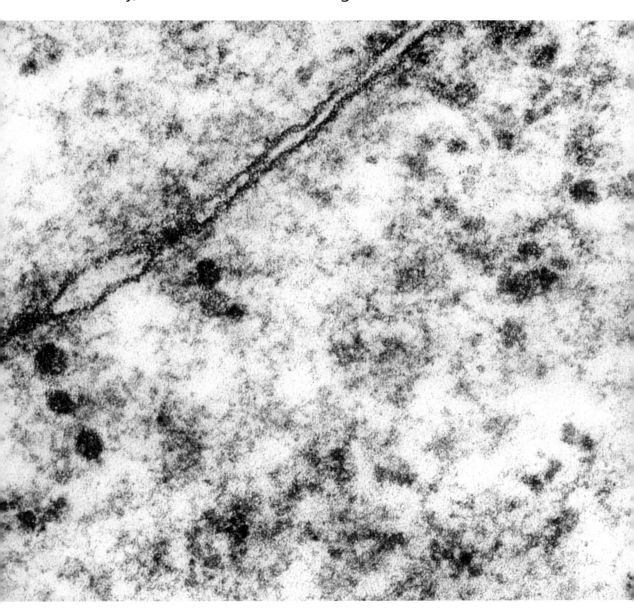

protein is copied from DNA to RNA, or ribonucleic acid, through a process called transcription. Like a messenger service, the code-carrying RNA then travels through pores in the nuclear membrane into the cytoplasm to structures called ribosomes, where proteins are made.

When RNA reaches one of these protein machines, the information from the gene copied by the RNA is read and interpreted, just as you are reading and understanding these words, in a process called translation. That information acts as text in an instruction manual. It tells the ribosome what ingredients are needed to make the desired protein and how to put them together. The ribosome functions like an assembly line in a factory, piecing together the protein step by step. The ingredients that make up proteins are called amino acids. Human cells use twenty amino acids. Some we make; others we must ingest.

Plant Cells v. Animal Cells

The cells of plants and animals share several traits but are different in important ways. Both have cell membranes and some of the same organelles. Both have nuclei containing DNA that can be translated into proteins. Plant cells, however, have a cell wall around their cell membranes. This wall gives rigidity and added protection to plant cells. When plant cells fill with water, they become stiff, which is called turgor pressure. If you have ever had a plant that was limp but became stiffer after you watered it, you have seen turgor pressure in action. Animal cells are far more flexible because they do not have a cell wall. But if they fill with too much water, they will burst and die. This process is known as cytolysis or osmotic lysis.

Using instructions from DNA, ribosomes make thousands of proteins by combining these twenty amino acids in different patterns. Some proteins made by a cell are used for jobs inside that cell. Others are put into packages and shipped out of the cell.

CHLOROPLASTS

Another important difference between plant and animal cells is how they obtain energy. Just as you need energy to walk and talk, cells need energy to perform their activities. Animals consume food for the energy needed to fuel cellular activity. Our cells must break down the carbohydrates, proteins, and fats we eat into glucose, which is used to produce an energy-storing molecule called adenosine triphosphate, or ATP. Any time a cell needs energy, a certain number of ATP molecules are cashed in by breaking them. When an ATP molecule is broken, energy is released. The cell uses this energy for all kinds of jobs, including movement, production of more cells, making proteins, and moving certain substances across the membrane. Just as a car requires a certain amount of gasoline to go a certain distance, a cell needs a certain amount of energy to carry out its functions.

Plant cells have special organelles called chloroplasts that allow plants to make the ATP they need from energy that they harness from sunlight. This process is called photosynthesis. Imagine if instead of having to eat to obtain energy for your daily activities, all you had to do was sit in the sun. Chloroplasts contain chlorophyll, the chemical pigment that gives plants their green color. In the fall, when sunlight is less available, plants can no longer make chlorophyll and other pigments become more dominant, causing leaves to turn yellow, red, and orange.

MITOCHONDRIA

Eukaryotic cells, including human cells, contain mitochondria. These organelles are the powerhouses of cells because they are the place where cellular respiration, the complex process by which ATP is made, takes place. Muscle cells, which require lots of energy, have thousands of mitochondria floating in their cytoplasm. Hair and skin cells have few mitochondria because they do less work and require less energy.

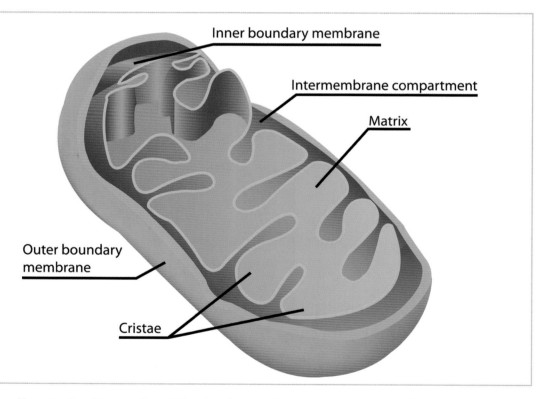

The mitochondria are where ATP molecules, a cell's energy source, are made. The multiple folds, or cristae, provide an enormous surface area on which that happens.

Unlike other organelles, mitochondria have two membranes, not one. The outer membrane of a mitochondrion covers the organelle. The inner membrane is repeatedly folded up inside the organelle to form cristae. Folding increases the amount of cristae and thus the amount of space available for the ATP-making process to occur. The more cristae mitochondria have, the more ATP, and thus the more energy, they can produce.

ENDOPLASMIC RETICULUM

The endoplasmic reticulum, or ER, is a complex organelle. It is membrane-bound and made of tubules that weave through the cytoplasm of eukaryotic cells. The ER usually touches both the nuclear membrane and the cell membrane. It functions as a large transport and packaging system.

There are two types of ERs. Rough ER has protein-assembling ribosomes attached to its surface, making it look bumpy. Proteins made by these ribosomes are inserted into the hollow tubes of the ER and sent through the cell to where they are needed using vesicles, just as a post office helps mail reach its final destination. Cells that make lots of protein have lots of rough ER. For example, pancreatic cells are full of rough ER. Pancreatic cells make insulin, which increases glucose uptake and storage.

Smooth ER does not have ribosomes attached to it and therefore looks smooth. One of its jobs is to make and break down certain large molecules. Liver cells, which break down toxins, have lots of smooth ER. Smooth ER is also a storage place for particles called ions, which are released when the cell needs them. Muscle cells need calcium ions to contract. These are released by the smooth ER when the muscle needs them. Smooth ER is also the place where lipids and steroids are synthesized and the attachment of receptors on cell membrane proteins occurs.

GOLGI APPARATUS

The Golgi apparatus is another important organelle found in many, but not all, eukaryotic cells. Like the ER, it is also comprised of numerous membrane stacks, known as cisternae. The Golgi apparatus is involved in modifying proteins and fats delivered from the ER by adding other molecules to them. One of its most crucial tasks is adding sugars to proteins, making them into glycoproteins. Imagine a car factory. If the ER is the site where the body, or skeleton, of the car is made, the Golgi is the place where specialized features are added on, like mirrors, doors, or brakes.

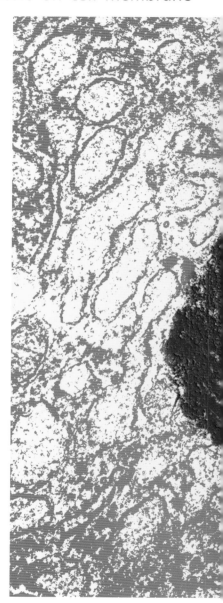

The Golgi apparatus helps modify, sort, and ship larger molecules to their final destinations inside or outside the cell. It can informally be thought of as a cellular post office.

VESICLES

The proteins, fats, and molecules created by the ER and the Golgi apparatus need a way to get from the places they are

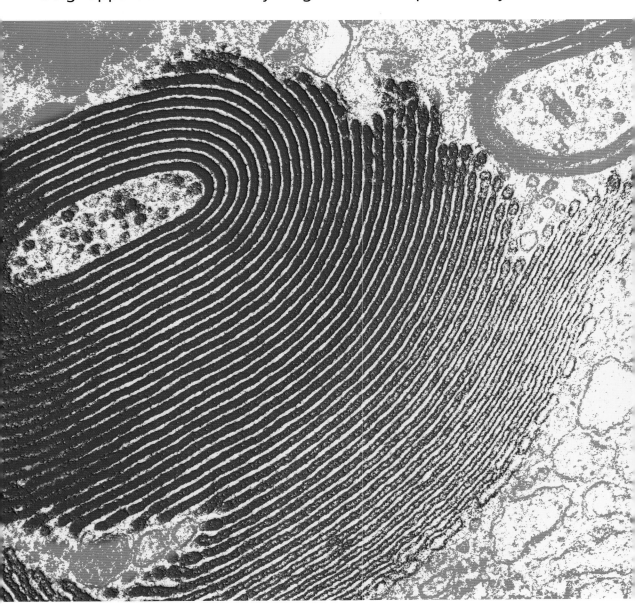

made to the places they are needed, whether inside or outside of the cell. The delivery vehicles of choice are often vesicles, which are bubblelike structures that "bud" out of the ER and Golgi membranes and fully surround their contents. Once released, the molecule-containing vesicles travel like a fleet of delivery trucks to the cell membrane for shipment out of the cell, or to other organelles where their contents are needed for a specific job. When a vesicle containing its cargo reaches its destination, its membrane joins with the membrane of the organelle or the cell's membrane, and its contents are released. Without the ability to form vesicles, molecules made by both the ER and the Golgi apparatus would never get to their destinations. Vacuoles are large vesicles that are also used to store molecules until they are needed.

LYSOSOMES AND PEROXISOMES

Lysosomes are similar to vesicles in that they are produced by budding from the ER and the Golgi apparatus. However, these structures contain digestive enzymes used to break down substances that the cell takes in through its membrane into usable nutrients and waste, just as the enzymes in your digestive system break down the foods you eat. Lysosomes can generally be viewed as cellular recycling centers.

Peroxisomes are special vesicles made by the ER that contain substances that break down poisonous wastes resulting from cellular activities. Examples of these dangerous substances are free radicals and hydrogen peroxide, which cause damage to DNA and other cell structures if they are not destroyed. Peroxisomes can be thought of as a cell's waste management system.

THE CYTOSKELETON

Your skeleton gives your body structure and support. It also helps you move. Cells have structures that perform similar functions. The cytoskeleton allows a cell to keep its three-dimensional shape. It also acts as a scaffold upon which vesicles and organelles can move. The cytoskeleton is made of three types of fibers. The first—fine, solid rods made of two twisted protein chains—are called microfilaments or actin filaments. The second are microtubules, which are hollow tubes. The third, the intermediate filaments, add strength to the cell's structure. Unlike your skeleton's constant and unchanging structure, the cytoskeleton can contract and expand, allowing cells to rearrange the contents of their cytoplasm in order to bring organelles closer together. The cytoskeletal fibers are also crucial to a cell's ability to divide and replicate, a process called mitosis.

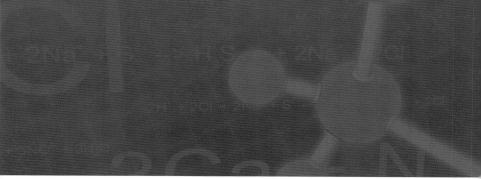

WHAT CELLS DO

We have learned that cells make proteins that are used in building cellular structures and performing cellular activities. We have also seen that our cells must convert the nutrients that we eat into a usable form of energy to power these activities. In order to perform any of these activities, however, there are many other things that cells must do.

Passive Transport

We know that the cell membrane acts as a barrier protecting the inside of the cell from the outside world. However, like all protective barriers, there must be ways for things to get in, such as nutrients, and out, such as waste. Just as security

The cell membrane is designed to keep harmful outside agents from entering the cell.
Sometimes, as this graphic illustrates, the membrane can't protect against invasion.

guards regulate who gets into and out of a given place, the properties of the cell membrane regulate what gets into and out of the cell.

The chemical properties of the cell membrane allow certain substances, like oxygen, carbon dioxide, and water, to pass through it freely. This process is called diffusion. Diffusion describes the tendency of substances to naturally move from an area of high concentration to an area of low concentration in an effort to seek equilibrium, or even distribution. For example, if someone on one side of a room sprays perfume, the scent will at first be very strong near that person and undetectable by someone on the other side of the room. Over time, however, the perfume molecules will spread out through the room, eventually leading to the detection of the scent by people on the other side. At the same time, people in the area where the perfume was first sprayed will notice that the scent becomes weaker. This is because the molecules will spread out evenly. That's diffusion.

Diffusion does not require the use of any energy and thus is a type of passive transport. The passive diffusion of water into and out of cells from areas of high to low concentration has a special name: osmosis. Diffusion can occur right through the membrane itself, through proteins that act as channels for molecules too large to squeeze between the molecules of the membrane itself, or with the assistance of carrier molecules that escort substances into and out of the cell by holding onto them.

ACTIVE TRANSPORT

Diffusion, however, cannot satisfy all of a cell's import and export needs. Sometimes, activities inside the cell require the

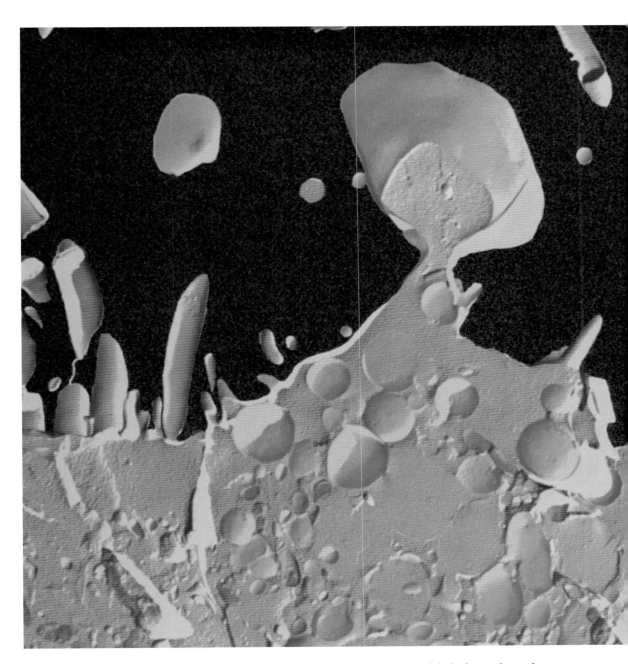

Mucus, secreted by upper airway cells, acts as a sticky barrier that traps debris, bacteria, and other inhaled substances. Hairlike projections called cilia help clear the debris-containing mucus.

movement of molecules from areas of low concentration to high concentration. This requires energy, or the use of ATP, to work against the natural tendency of substances to spread out evenly.

This is where other proteins in the cell membrane come into play. Proteins involved in active transport act as pumps, driving specific substances into and out of the cell. One well-known

Cellular Communication

Just as you receive and interpret signals from your environment through sight, touch, smell, sound, and taste as a way to understand your surroundings and communicate with others, your cells communicate with each other and their immediate environments, too. Cells must do this without the receptors that we have come to rely on, namely our ears, nose, eyes, skin, and tongue.

Cells have other kinds of receptors that help them pick up, interpret, and respond to information from their surroundings. This process is known as cell signaling. It can occur between cells that are near each other or far away. It can occur between cells of the same type or of different types. Some cells respond to touch and will stop growing when they come in contact with nearby cells—this type of signaling is known as juxtacrine signaling. Some release chemical signals when they detect disease-causing germs, causing other cells to attack.

Nerve cells communicate using electrical and chemical signals. If you touch a hot stove, the sensory nerves in your hand must quickly send a message to your brain. Like a game of telephone, these sensory messages are passed along chains of nerve cells until they reach the brain, where the signal is translated as "hot." The brain then sends another signal back to the motor neurons and muscles of your hand instructing it to move.

All of this happens very quickly and without you even thinking about it. If this cellular communication is interrupted, however, by disease or injury, there will be no signal telling your hand that the stove is hot or to move it to prevent it from getting burned.

example is the pump responsible for pushing sodium out of the cell and potassium into the cell. If these pumps failed, sodium would rush into the cell and potassium would rush out, disrupting important cellular activities.

Some cells will bring in large particles or even entire other cells by temporarily breaking their membrane, surrounding the desired substance with a vesicle, and reforming the membrane around it. This engulfing process, called endocytosis, requires energy. Exocytosis, the removal of large and unwanted substances from inside the cell, involves the opposite process. Vesicles containing waste products will merge with the cell membrane and dump their contents outside the cell in a manner that does not contaminate the inside of the cell.

GETTING AROUND

We already know that the cytoskeleton is important in maintaining cell shape and structure. In some cells, however, parts of the cytoskeleton can break down and rebuild, allowing the whole cell to move. This process is called cell crawling. In some cells, microtubules are arranged into long, whiplike tails, or flagella, which help propel the cell through watery environments. Human sperm cells have flagella that help them swim. Other cells have cilia, which are shorter hairlike projections made of microtubules that cover the surface of a cell and allow movement. Cilia are also important for moving substances across the surface of some cells. Cells inside our upper airway have cilia that wave back and forth to move mucus and debris away from our lungs.

Making More Cells

Like all other living things, cells eventually die. For this reason, cells must reproduce, or make more of themselves so that the body can keep functioning. Another reason why cells must reproduce is so that an organism, like an animal or plant, can grow. Cells also reproduce in order to replace damaged or ill cells. Some cells in your body reproduce quickly, like the cells of your stomach lining that are constantly eaten away by the acid used to help digest food. Skin cells are another example of rapidly reproducing cells. Other cells reproduce slowly, only under certain circumstances, or not at all, such as bone, nerve, and brain cells. Whereas a cut on your hand will heal fairly quickly, damage to the brain heals very slowly and sometimes not at all.

Cells reproduce by dividing through a process called mitosis. In order for this to occur, a cell must first copy all of its DNA so that the new cells produced have all of the information they need to function properly. One cell, called a parent cell, will duplicate its DNA and divide it and all of its organelles evenly before the cell divides into identical daughter cells.

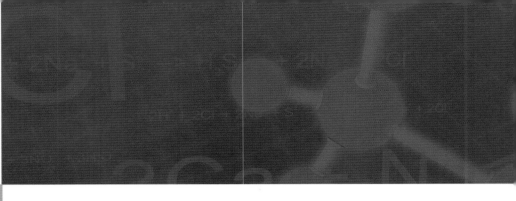

3

MAJOR MILESTONES IN CELL BIOLOGY

In 1665, scientist Robert C. Hooke was the first person to see a cell and recognize it as the basic building block of life. Looking at a thin slice of cork with a compound microscope—an instrument that uses two or more lenses to form enlarged images of very small objects—Hooke saw small, regularly spaced, boxlike structures surrounded by well-defined walls. Because these spaces reminded him of the small rooms that monks lived in, Hooke called them cellulae, from the Latin word *cella*, or "little room." What he actually saw were the cell walls of the dead cork plant cells. Hooke went on to write a detailed book, *Micrographia*, published in 1665, about all of his observations through the microscope.

In 1674, scientist Antoni van Leeuwenhoek was the first person to observe a living cell. While looking at a drop of water under a handheld microscope that he had designed, he saw what he described as swimming "animalcules." These likely belonged to the single-celled protozoa *Spirogyra*, an algae. Later, with improvements to the microscope, many of which he designed himself, Leeuwenhoek was also the first to see bacterial cells.

RECOGNIZING THE NUCLEUS

In 1831, botanist Robert Brown was the first person to use the term "nucleus", Latin for "little nut," to describe what many scientists had noticed for years without recognizing its importance. While studying orchid cells, Brown noted that they contained a small, opaque "spot." Importantly, he also noted that many different cell types contained a nucleus and theorized that the nucleus may have something to do with cellular reproduction.

Robert Brown, the first person to describe the cell's nucleus in 1831, also described what is now called Brownian movement, the random, zigzag movement of small particles in fluid.

Looking at Cells

Most cells are so small that they cannot be seen with the human eye—not without assistance, that is. Some bacterial cells are so small that one thousand of them lined up equals only the width of a single human hair. Imagine, then, how small the organelles within these cells are. In order to see and study cells, scientists use microscopes, which are devices that can magnify small things up to twenty million times.

There are several types of microscopes. Light microscopes—the ones you are most likely to use in your science class—use light and lenses to magnify an image up to one thousand times, but only in two dimensions. The most commonly used light microscope is the compound microscope, which has two or more lenses.

Some cells are still too small to be seen with a light microscope, so a more powerful microscope must be used. Instead of using light, electron microscopes use a beam of charged particles to create an image of cells in two or three dimensions. They can magnify up to twenty million times, are far more complicated and expensive to use and maintain, and usually require very special and specific laboratory conditions in order to work properly.

DEBUNKING SPONTANEOUS GENERATION

For almost two thousand years, it was believed that living things arose from nonliving organic matter. This theory, called spontaneous generation, was first put forth by the highly respected Greek philosopher Aristotle. It helped make sense of what was not yet understood about the microscopic world of cells. The theory was thought to explain how maggots could appear on a piece of spoiled meat and mice would appear from wheat grains that sat too long in a bucket outside. How else could these living things get there unless something in the meat or

One of the founding fathers of microbiology, Louis Pasteur helped prove that cells can only come from other cells and that microorganisms, like bacteria, are the cause of many diseases.

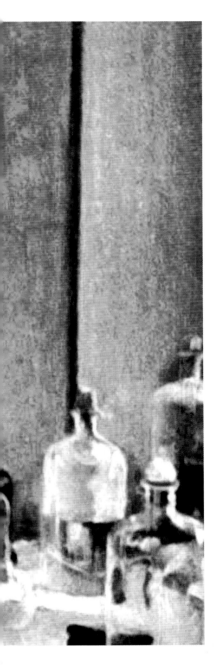

the wheat kernels and a "life force" came together spontaneously to create life where there appeared to be none before? Thanks to the work of scientists Francesco Redi in the 1600s, Lazzaro Spallanzani in the 1700s, John Needham, and ultimately Louis Pasteur, with his famous "swan-necked flask experiment," in the 1800s, we now know that life comes only from other life and cells only from other cells.

THE CELL THEORY OF LIFE

Closing the door on the era of spontaneous generation opened the door to the next obvious questions: what is the smallest possible unit of life, and what defines "alive"? It wasn't until 1839 that a theory was formulated in an attempt to answer such questions.

In 1838, botanist Matthias Schleiden theorized that all the parts of a plant are made of cells or the product of cells. One year later, zoologist Theodor Schwann stated that "there is one universal principle of development for the elementary parts of organisms...and this principle is in the formation of cells." Today, the cell theory first put forth by Schleiden and Schwann is still the basis for our modern understanding of cell biology. Simply put, it states that:

1. All living things are made from one or more cells
2. Cells arise from preexisting cells
3. The cell is the smallest unit of life

In the 1850s, doctors Robert Remak and Rudolf Virchow showed that cells are formed from the division of preexisting cells. Or, in other words, all cells come from other cells. Virchow also developed the notion that illness and disease must be a result of negative changes in cells, though it would be years before scientists would learn that bacteria and other organisms are often the cause of these changes. Over time, with improvements in microscope technology and techniques for staining different parts of the cells, the various organelles were more readily seen and identified, leading to the study of their functions.

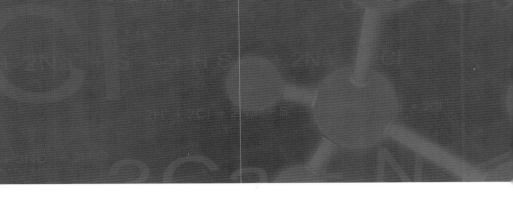

RECENT BREAKTHROUGHS AND EMERGING DEVELOPMENTS

While scientists like Schleiden, Schwann, Virchow, and Hooke helped lay the foundation for our modern understanding of cell biology, not all of what we know about cell biology was discovered hundreds of years ago. In the last one hundred years, our understanding of cells has grown extensively due to continuously improving technology that allows us to see deeper into the heart of cells and expand experimentation in the laboratory.

UNRAVELING THE STRUCTURE OF DNA

Although DNA was isolated in the late 1800s, it was only in 1953 that the structure of the molecule that

James Watson and Francis Crick were awarded the Nobel Prize, an honor shared with Albert Einstein, for revealing the structure of DNA, a discovery that changed the world.

carries all of our genetic information and acts as a blueprint for building an organism was finally understood. Two scientists, Francis Crick and James Watson, were the first to unravel the structure of DNA. They did so by literally building it out of large cardboard cutouts representing the molecule's different components and fitting them together like puzzle pieces. They were the first to prove that DNA is a double helix (two strands twisted together), that it contains genes on the inside of the helix, and that it can "unzip" to copy itself. In 1962, their achievement earned them a Nobel Prize, one of the highest scientific honors in the world. The understanding of DNA's structure has helped scientists understand how genes are passed from generation to generation, the causes for many genetic illnesses, how proteins are made, and how species differ.

Stem Cells

Another important modern achievement in cell biology has been research involving stem cells. Embryonic stem cells are active during the early development of organisms, including you. You began

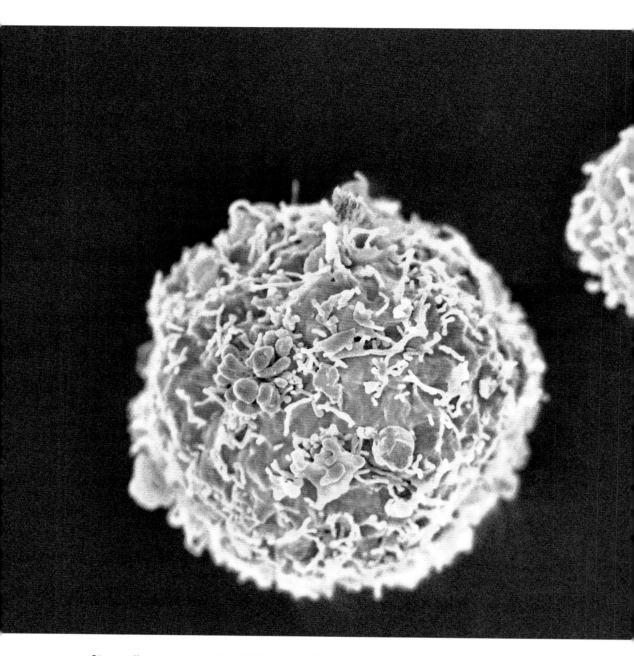

Stem cells are unspecialized "blank slates" that, under certain conditions in the body, can be triggered to become cells with specific functions.

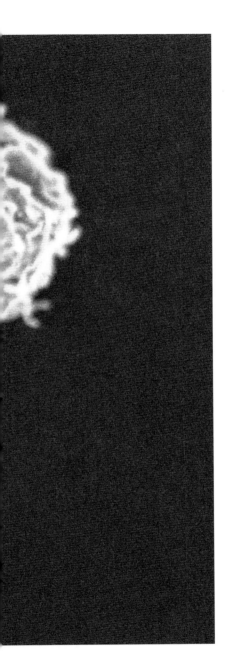

your life as a single cell that divided and divided and divided, resulting in a cluster of eight, fifty, then thousands of cells. Today, your body is made of trillions of cells, many of which are highly specialized and have very specific jobs. Most of them arose from those unspecialized embryonic stem cells, which have the incredible ability to develop into almost any type of body cell, including bone, muscle, nerve, and skin. Amazingly, researchers have also found that many adult tissues contain stem cells, though they appear to be slightly more limited in their ability to become other types of cells. The role of adult stem cells is to maintain and repair the tissues in which they are found. Bone marrow, for example, contains adult stem cells that serve to replace all the different types of blood cells when they die or are damaged.

Researchers have been trying to figure out how stem cells "know" what cells to become and what information, or growth factors, direct their development. If we could learn how to obtain or create cells that have the ability to become any type of cell, we may be able to treat or perhaps cure many diseases simply by creating healthy versions of sick or damaged cells.

Imagine that you have a disease or suffer an injury that causes your heart muscle cells not to work properly and perhaps causes your heart to stop beating. If somehow deprogrammed stem cells could be transplanted into your heart muscle and triggered to develop, or differentiate, into healthy heart muscle cells, your disease might be cured. While wonderful in theory, this kind of research is in its very early stages. But advances are made daily, giving researchers hope that one day these techniques can be used widely.

Competition in the Lab

The achievements of Watson and Crick relied heavily on the work of scientist Rosalind Franklin, who had used a special technology, X-ray diffraction, to capture an image of the shape of DNA. At the time, Franklin was one of the very few women in her field. Her now-famous X-ray photograph was shown to Watson and Crick without her permission by another scientist who disliked her but worked for the same research team.

It was this image that gave the two men the "eureka" moment that ultimately allowed them to figure out and build the specific structure of DNA using 3-D cardboard models. They shared the Nobel Prize with Maurice Wilkins, the scientist who showed them Franklin's photograph. There has been much debate about whether Franklin, too, should have received the Nobel Prize for her crucial contribution to Watson and Crick's discovery. Sadly, however, she died at age thirty-seven, never finding out that Watson and Crick had seen her unpublished photograph and that this helped them change history.

A Heated Debate

Stem cell research has been very controversial, particularly when it comes to embryonic stem cells. Currently, the only way to obtain embryonic stem cells, which have the most potential to become any type of cell, is to remove them from embryos that are a few days old or from fetuses that are a few weeks old, a process that can destroy the embryo or fetus. Some believe this is the same as destroying a person. Others feel that while the embryo and fetus have the potential to become a person if allowed to fully develop, they are not yet people and it is wrong not to do research that might result in techniques that may prevent, treat, or cure deadly illnesses.

There are many interesting and valid arguments on both sides of the debate, one of which asks: When does personhood really begin? At birth? At the one-cell stage? Somewhere in between?

One hope for many scientists is that this complicated issue may one day be avoided completely if we learn to reprogram adult stem cells back to a state in which they can become any cells instead of just certain types of cells, or if we can find adult stem cells in all human tissue types.

Cloning

Mammals, including humans, reproduce by sexual reproduction. When humans mate, a sperm cell with genes from the male meets an egg cell with genes from the female. These randomly combine to create an embryo that later becomes a baby whose genes are a combination of its mother's and father's genes. You might be tall like your mom and have blue eyes like your father, but you are not identical to either of them. A clone, on the other hand, is an exact genetic copy of a single

parent. Many bacteria reproduce this way. Identical twins are genetic clones, too, sharing the exact same DNA.

In 1996, after more than 275 attempts, Dr. Ian Wilmut and his team of researchers created the world's first clone of an adult mammal, a sheep named Dolly. Wilmut removed the nucleus from a cell of a six-year-old sheep. As we know, the nucleus of a cell contains all of that animal's genes, tightly wrapped up in DNA. Next, Wilmut took the nucleus and placed it inside the egg cell of a female sheep after taking out its nucleus. He then used chemical and electrical signals to trigger the egg cell with the donated adult sheep cell nucleus to start dividing as it normally would after meeting with a sperm from a male sheep. The egg cell was placed into the womb of another female sheep, where it became an embryo. Eventually, a lamb was born that was an exact genetic copy, a clone, of the adult sheep that donated its nucleus. Since then, other mammals have been cloned in this way,

The birth of Dolly, the first cloned sheep, caused international excitement and concern. Today, the cloning debate continues. There is much controversy over cloning animals and other organisms, including humans.

including cows, goats, and mice. The technology is still far from perfect, and usually there are many failures before success.

While the birth of Dolly was a huge milestone in the fields of cell biology, genetics, and reproduction, there has been much debate about the possible dangers of this technology. Medically, we don't yet know what problems a cloned animal might have or what illnesses it may be vulnerable to because its DNA comes from an adult cell that may be damaged due to age.

We know that Dolly lived to be only six and that many cloned animals have been born with birth defects. There are many ethical debates about cloning as well. What if such technology was used to clone a human? Would a cloned human have issues of identity? Is cloning "playing God" or disturbing the natural order of life? What if someone wanted to clone humans with specific characteristics thought to be more desirable, such as intelligence or physical strength?

GENETIC THERAPY

Our understanding of cell biology, the inner workings of the nucleus, and DNA has led to studies of gene mutation, or damage, and the desire to fix this damage. If you wanted to bake cookies and there was a typo in a recipe that you were using, or worse yet, the word "flour" were missing or changed to something else like "ketchup," the cookies would probably not come out as you hoped. Now imagine the instructions for building a car were missing the parts for brakes or a steering wheel. Not only will this car not function correctly, it will likely be very dangerous to drive. Perhaps it will not work at all.

We know that genes code for proteins that are crucial to cellular function. If a gene is damaged, or part or all of it is missing, the protein that it codes for will be made incorrectly, just like the car in the previous example, or it may not be made at all.

Many gene mutations have no effect. To use our baking example, if the word "flour" were written "flourrr," you would still read the recipe correctly. However, some gene mutations are very dangerous, as in the example of a car missing its brakes. In fact, there are many diseases we have come

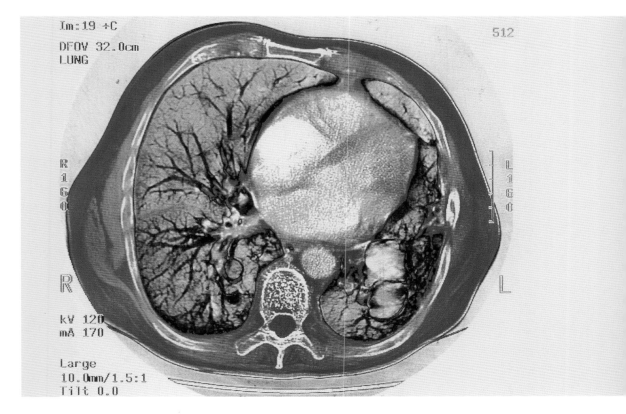

People with the lung disease cystic fibrosis rarely live past their late thirties. Gene therapy could provide a treatment or perhaps a cure for this and other tragic illnesses.

to understand are a result of gene mutations. Some of these mutations we are born with—we inherited them from our parents. Others are acquired over time, having slipped through a cell's remarkable mechanisms for proofreading genes and fixing mistakes. Either way, many of these gene mutations are deadly or can make you very sick.

In the last few decades, scientists have been experimenting with gene therapy in the hopes of repairing or replacing damaged genes with copies that are undamaged and code for the correct proteins. For example, cystic fibrosis, a disease that causes damage to the lungs and digestive systems, is caused by damage to a particular gene. People with this illness have a lowered life expectancy of 37.4 years. Scientists have been working on delivering working copies of the gene to the lung cells where the correct proteins can be made, thereby eliminating or reducing the symptoms of cystic fibrosis. The tricky thing has been getting the gene into the right cells, then getting it into the DNA. Believe it or not, scientists have been using the virus that causes the common cold as a delivery system for these valuable genetic packages. The virus is modified so as not to make people sick.

5

EVERYDAY CELL BIOLOGY

W hile you might think that cell biology is interesting, you may still be wondering how the information we learn about cells and their properties might affect you on a daily basis. You might be surprised.

THE IMMUNE SYSTEM

Understanding cell biology has helped scientists understand the nature of infection, or how we get sick. Rudolf Virchow had it right in the 1850s when he theorized that illness may be the result of sick cells. For example, when you get the flu, this is actually the result of the influenza virus. When you inhale the virus after being around someone with the flu, the virus sticks to the cells in your nose, throat, or lungs. The virus enters the cell membrane. Once inside, the virus "tricks" the infected cell into making thousands of copies of its genetic information and its parts, which are then assembled into thousands of brand-new influenza viruses.

In this way, a single flu virus can hijack a cell's protein-making machinery and use it to its advantage. Thousands of new viruses burst out of the infected cell's membrane in a process called lysis. These new viruses go on to infect nearby

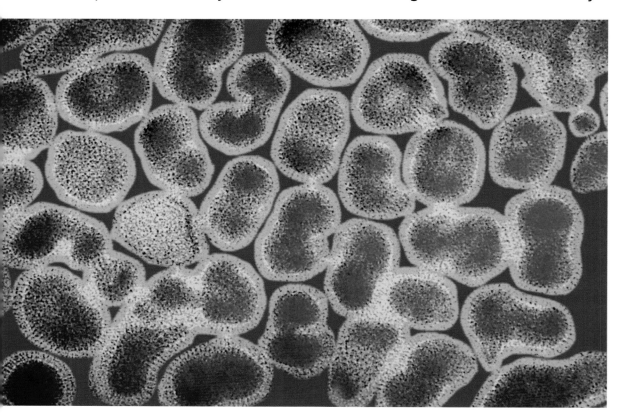

The influenza virus changes, or mutates, rapidly. For this reason, the flu vaccine your doctor gave you this year won't protect you from next year's flu virus.

cells, where the process begins again. You can see how inhaling only a few influenza viruses can lead to millions of viruses very quickly, many of which will be expelled in your coughs or sneezes and infect those around you. Viruses are not alone in their ability to make us sick. Bacteria, fungi, and other microorganisms can make us ill, too.

Our understanding of cell biology has helped us learn how the human body fights infection. When you have the flu, you will eventually feel better. This is because your body has special cells that fight viral infections. When you have strep throat, a condition caused by a specific kind of bacteria, other types of special cells come to the rescue. All of these illness-fighting cells are part of your immune system, which is a series of responses that your body has to foreign invaders like viruses and bacteria.

Key players in this response are white blood cells. Neutrophils are the most common type of white blood cell and are important in fighting bacterial infection. They travel in the bloodstream, waiting for signals that infection has occurred. When cells are infected with disease-causing bacteria, they release chemical signals that trigger neutrophils to come to the rescue. The neutrophils follow these signals to the site of infection, where they eat the offending bacteria by phagocytosis, send signals to call in other immune cells, and release substances that help destroy bacteria invaders. There are many other types of white blood cells, some of which are better at fighting viral, fungal, or parasitic infections. Ultimately, the cells of the immune system all work together to protect us from infection.

Understanding the immune system has helped us develop vaccines to prevent illnesses and antibiotics to help treat them. Vaccines contain part of a virus, a bacterium, or a weakened or dead version of it that cannot make you sick but will trigger an immune response, calling the white blood cells to action. When your immune system finds an infectious agent, it makes an antibody to it. The next time your cells are infected by that same infectious agent, the antibodies to that germ will recognize and remove it before it can make you sick. Antibiotics, on the other hand, are given when certain bacteria have already infected you. When you have strep throat, your doctor will give you an antibiotic that targets the invading bacteria and kills it or prevents it from multiplying. Antibiotics do not work on viruses.

Understanding Our Origins

Did you know that studying cells can help us understand where we came from? While the nucleus of our cells contains most of our DNA, a small piece of DNA exists in our cellular mitochondria, the organelle that converts energy from food into ATP, the form of energy that cells can use. This small piece of DNA is inherited from our mothers, not our fathers, because of how human reproduction occurs. It changes only as a result of random mutation, just like regular DNA. Scientists can use mitochondrial DNA to trace our ancestry by comparing samples of this DNA from different people. People whose mitochondrial DNA share the same unique characteristics or mutations are likely related. Analysis of mitochondrial DNA is being used to trace our ancestry back more than two hundred thousand years to the first human female from whom we are all descended. In scientific circles, she is called Mitochondrial Eve.

CELLULAR AGING

All living things grow old, including our cells. But why? One reason is telomere shortening. A telomere is a repeating segment of DNA at the end of chromosomes that protects the important parts of the chromosome from damage during replication. When cells divide, the chromosomes are copied completely, but the telomeres are not. As a result, these protective ends get shorter each time the cell divides until they are so short that the cell will no longer divide. One theory states that the reason mammals, including humans, age is because as the years pass, the telomeres of more and more of our cells shorten to the point that our cells no longer divide, making repair of tissues, defense against disease, and maintenance of normal tissue function difficult.

CANCER: CELLS OUT OF CONTROL

We know that like all living things, cells get old, sick, and even die. For that reason, many of the cells in the body make more of themselves by dividing to replace old or damaged cells. This process is usually very orderly and controlled. Cancer occurs when this orderly, controlled process goes wrong. This is often caused by damage to a cell's DNA that disturbs normal cell growth and division. This damage can be inherited or acquired. We know, for example, that smoking cigarettes can cause cancer. Sometimes, people get cancer for no clear reason.

There are many types of cancer—some that grow quickly and some that grow slowly. Cancer is much more common in

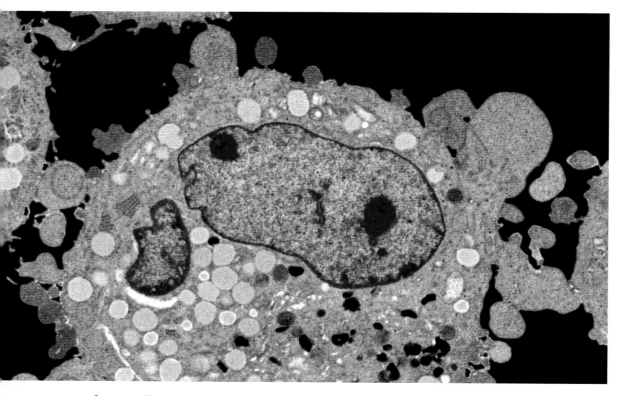

Cancer cells grow uncontrollably and do not self-destruct as many normal cells do when damaged. Cancer treatments involve the use of drugs, radiation, surgery, and chemotherapy.

older people than in younger people and children. Cancer is not contagious, like the flu or a cold.

Normally, damaged cells die, or self-destruct. In the case of cancer, the damaged cells do not die but continue to grow and make more damaged copies of themselves. This results in a mass of cells, called a tumor. Tumors can grow so big that they can invade nearby tissues, causing problems there. Sometimes, cancerous cells break off the tumor and travel to other parts of the body in the blood or lymphatic system. Wherever they wind up, they will continue to divide and create tumors in those locations. This is called metastasis. Researchers are constantly studying cancer in an effort to find better treatments and a cure.

GENETIC ENGINEERING

Like gene therapy, genetic engineering involves the altering of DNA by inserting genes that code for certain proteins. Just as the influenza virus can trick our cells into making viral proteins, scientists have been able to insert certain genes into various cell types to make them perform a desired function or produce a certain substance that they otherwise would not be able to.

For example, people with diabetes do not make enough insulin, the substance that helps get sugars we eat into our cells where it can be used to make ATP for energy. Diabetics need to inject insulin so that their cells can function. But where does it all come from? Scientists have been able to remove the insulin gene from human cells and

Crops genetically engineered to need less water may allow farming in arid parts of the world. They may also pose unforeseen threats to the environment and human health.

place it into the DNA of a particular type of bacteria called *E. coli*. The bacteria read the insulin gene and produce it as if the gene were part of its own DNA. The insulin is then collected from the bacterial cells and used in the production of insulin injections for diabetics.

How does one bacterial cell make enough insulin? It doesn't. Bacterial cells reproduce very quickly, and one cell can give rise to hundreds of thousands in very little time. Each bacterial cell carrying the inserted insulin gene will pass the gene along to its offspring, resulting in millions of insulin-producing cells. In this way, scientists have turned bacteria into insulin-producing factories.

Other forms of genetic engineering involve inserting genes into vegetables and other plants. For example, some corn species have been genetically altered to produce substances toxic to insects that would otherwise destroy the corn. Some rice has also been genetically modified to contain vitamin A, which is limited in some areas of the world but is still needed for health. Other crops have been modified to resist drought, which might be the answer to failed farming in desert areas. In fact, 60 to 70 percent of the food at your supermarket is likely genetically modified. Genetically modified foods have been another topic of much debate. Some people fear that these foods aren't natural and might be dangerous to humans. Some fear that traits like pest resistance might spread to undesirable plants, such as weeds. The technology is still new. Therefore, we still cannot be sure what the long-term effects of genetic engineering are.

GLOSSARY

active transport Transport of a substance across a cell membrane that requires an expenditure of energy.

antibiotic A drug used to treat infections caused by bacteria and other microorganisms.

antibody A protein made by the immune system that recognizes and helps fight infections and other foreign substances in the body.

ATP (adenosine triphosphate) The energy-yielding molecule in cells that is used to fuel chemical reactions.

chlorophyll A green pigment in plants that converts energy from sunlight into chemical energy through the process of photosynthesis.

chloroplast A plant organelle where photosynthesis takes place.

chromosome A structure of compacted, intertwined molecules of DNA in the nucleus of cells that carry the cell's genetic information. Humans have forty-six chromosomes.

DNA (deoxyribonucleic acid) A molecule that contains the genetic instructions used in the development and functioning of all known living organisms and some viruses.

eukaryotic cell A cell with a membrane-bound nucleus and organelles.

gene A segment of DNA that carries the genetic information necessary for the production of a protein.

gene therapy A technique of replacing disease-causing genes with normal ones.

genetic engineering Altering the DNA of a cell to make it capable of performing a desired task, such as producing certain substances.

mitochondrial DNA DNA thought to be passed down from the first human female from whom we are all descended.

mitochondrion An organelle containing enzymes responsible for producing energy.

nucleoid The part of the prokaryotic cell that contains DNA.

photosynthesis A process requiring chlorophyll by which plants capture and use sunlight to make food and build stores of energy.

prokaryotic cell A cell that does not have a nucleus or membrane-bound organelles.

RNA (ribonucleic acid) A molecule made from DNA that is involved in making proteins.

transcription The process involving the copying of genetic data from DNA to RNA.

translation The process by which a protein is made from the information contained in a molecule of messenger RNA.

vaccine A substance given to help the body make antibodies and provide protection against a disease; it is made from the virus or bacteria that causes the disease.

white blood cell A cell of the immune system that is important in defending the body against infectious disease and foreign materials.

FOR MORE INFORMATION

American Society for Cell Biology
8120 Woodmont Avenue, Suite 750
Bethesda, MD 20814-2762
(301) 347-9300
Web site: http://www.ascb.org
The American Society for Cell Biology strives to
bring the varied facets of cell biology together
to promote and develop the field of cell
biology.

American Society of Gene and Cell Therapy
555 East Wells Street, Suite 1100
Milwaukee, WI 53202
(414) 278-1341
Web site: http://www.asgct.org
This scientific organization is dedicated to the
understanding, development, and application of
genetic and cellular therapies and the promotion
of education in the field.

Canadian Bioethics Society
561 Rocky Ridge Bay NW
Calgary, AB T3G 4E7
Canada
(403) 208-8027
Web site: http://www.bioethics.ca

This is a forum for professionals interested in sharing ideas relating to bioethics and finding solutions to bioethical problems.

Health Canada—Office of Biotechnology and Science
Postal Locator 0702A
Ottawa, ON K1A 0L2
Canada
(613) 957-0346
Web site: http://www.hc-sc.gc.ca/sr-sr/biotech/index-eng.php
This Canadian organization communicates with the public about health promotion, disease prevention, and safety.

National Cancer Institute
NCI Public Inquiries Office
6116 Executive Boulevard, Room 3036A
Bethesda, MD 20892-8322
(800) 422-6237
Web site: http://www.cancer.gov
The National Cancer Institute is dedicated to cancer research and education.

WEB SITES

Due to the changing nature of Internet links, Rosen Publishing has developed an online list of Web sites related to the subject of this book. This site is updated regularly. Please use this link to access the list:

http://www.rosenlinks.com/sms/cell

FOR FURTHER READING

Arato, Rona. *Protists: Algae, Amoeba, Plankton, and Other Protists*. New York, NY: Crabtree Publishing Company, 2010.

Ballard, Carol. *Cells and Cell Function*. New York, NY: Rosen Publishing Group, 2010.

Biskup, Agnieszka. *Understanding Viruses with Max Axiom, Super Scientist*. Mankato, MN: Graphic Library, 2010.

Cregan, Elizabeth, and Bradford Kendall. *Pioneers in Cell Biology*. Minneapolis, MN: Compass Point Books, 2010.

Giddings, Sharon. *Cystic Fibrosis* (Genes and Disease). New York, NY: Chelsea House, 2009.

Hamilton, Gina. *Kingdoms of Life: Monera*. Dayton, OH: Milliken Publishing Company, 2006.

Hodge, Russ. *Developmental Biology: From a Cell to an Organism*. New York, NY: Facts on File, 2009.

Hodge, Russ. *Genetic Engineering*. New York, NY: Facts on File, 2009.

Keyser, Amber. *Decoding Genes with Max Axion, Super Scientist*. Mankato, MN: Graphic Library, 2010.

Latham, Donna. *Cells, Tissues and Organs*. Milwaukee, WI: Raintree, 2008.

McManus, Lori. *Cell Function and Specialization*. Milwaukee, WI: Raintree, 2008.

McManus, Lori. *Cell Systems*. Portsmouth, NH: Heinemann, 2010.

Oxlade, Chris, and Corinne Stockley. *The World of the Microscope*. London, England: Usborne Books, 2008.

Panno, Joseph. *Animal Cloning*. New York, NY: Facts on File, 2010.

Panno, Joseph. *Gene Therapy*. New York, NY: Facts on File, 2010.

Parker, Steven. *Molds, Mushrooms & Other Fungi*. Mankato, MN: Compass Point Books, 2009.

Somerville, Barbara Ann. *Animal Cells and Life Processes*. Portsmouth, NH: Heinemann, 2010.

Somerville, Barbara Ann. *Cells and Disease*. Portsmouth, NH: Heinemann, 2010.

Taylor, Barbara. *Interactive Explorer: Animal Kingdom*. San Diego, CA: Silver Dolphin Books, 2010.

Walker, Denise. *Cells and Life Processes*. London, England: Evans Brothers, Ltd., 2010.

BIBLIOGRAPHY

Alberts, Bruce, Alexander Johnson, Julian Lewis, and
Martin Raff. *Molecular Biology of the Cell*. 5th ed.
New York, NY: Garland Science, 2008.

Bauman, Robert. *Microbiology: With Diseases
by Taxonomy*. San Francisco, CA: Benjamin
Cummings, 2007.

Beauchamp, Thomas, LeRoy Walters, Jeffrey Kahn,
and Anna Mastroianni. *Contemporary Issues
in Bioethics*. 7th ed. Beverly, MA: Wadsworth
Publishing, 2007.

Hodge, Russ. *Human Genetics* (Genetics and
Evolution). New York, NY: Facts On File, 2010

Hooke, Robert. *Micrographia or Some Physiological
Descriptions of Minute Bodies*. New York, NY:
Cosimo Classics, 2007.

Karp, Gerald. *Cell and Molecular Biology: Concepts
and Experiments*. Hoboken, NJ: Wiley, 2009.

Kole, Chittaranjan. *Transgenic Crop Plants: Volume
1: Principles and Development*. New York, NY:
Springer, 2010.

Maddox, Brenda. *Rosalind Franklin: The Dark Lady of
DNA*. New York, NY: HarperCollins, 2002.

Mazzarello, Paolo. "A Unifying Concept: The History
of Cell Theory." Nature.com, 1999. Retrieved
March 12, 2010 (http://www.nature.com/ncb/
journal/v1/n1/full/ncb0599_E13.html).

Nova. "The Cloning Process." PBS.org. Retrieved March 21, 2010 (http://www.pbs.org/wgbh/nova/sciencenow/3209/04-clon-nf.html).

Nova. *Cracking the Code of Life*. Video. WGBH Educational Foundation and Clear Blue Sky Productions, 2001.

Royston, Angela. *Colds, the Flu, and Other Infections* (How's Your Health?). Mankato, MN: Smart Apple Media, 2008.

Sanders, Robert. "'Evolved' Virus May Improve Gene Therapy for Cystic Fibrosis." Berkeley.edu, February 17, 2009. Retrieved March 8, 2010 (http://berkeley.edu/news/media/releases/2009/02/17_schaffer.shtml).

Schultz, Mark. *The Stuff of Life. A Graphic Guide to Genetics and DNA*. New York, NY: Hill and Wang, 2009.

Sompayrac, Lauren. *How Pathogenic Viruses Work*. Sudbury, MA: Jones and Bartlett Publishers, Inc., 2002.

Sykes, Bryan. *The Seven Daughters of Eve*. New York, NY: Norton, 2001.

Thomas, Christopher Scott. *Stem Cell Now*. New York, NY: Plume, 2006.

Weinberg, Robert. *The Biology of Cancer*. New York, NY: Garland Science, 2006.

INDEX

About the Author

Aubrey Stimola has a degree in bioethics from Bard College and a master's degree in physician assistant sciences from Albany Medical College. She has worked for a nonprofit public health organization in Manhattan and the New York State Department of Health and currently practices emergency medicine in Saratoga Springs, New York, as a physician assistant.

Photo Credits